BIRD VIEWING AREAS

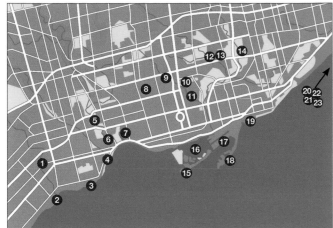

1. Etobicoke Creek Valley
2. Marie Curtis Park
3. Colonel Samuel Smith Park
4. Humber Bay Park
5. Lambton Woods Park
6. Humber River Marshes
7. High Park
8. Cedarvale Ravine
9. Beltline Ravine
10. Mount Pleasant Cemetery
11. Moore Park
12. Sunnybrook Park
13. Wilket Creek Park
14. Charles Sauriol Conservation Reserve
15. Toronto Islands
16. Toronto Bay & Harbour
17. Cherry Beach
18. Tommy Thompson Park/ Leslie Street Spit
19. Ashbridge's Bay Park
20. Highland Creek
21. Pickering Marsh
22. Squires Beach
23. Rouge River Mouth

Most illustrations show the adult male in breeding coloration. Colors and markings may be duller or absent during different seasons. The measurements denote the length of most species from bill to tail tip. Illustrations are not to scale.

Waterford Press publishes reference guides that introduce readers to nature observation, outdoor recreation and survival skills. Product information is featured on the website: www.waterfordpress.com.

Text & illustrations © 2013, 2022 Waterford Press Inc. All rights reserved. Photos © iStock Photo. Ecoregion map © The National Atlas of the United States. To order or for information or custom published products please call 800-434-2555 or email orderdesk@waterfordpress.com. For permissions or to share comments email editor@waterfordpress.com. 2202017

ISBN 978-1-58355-789-1
50795
UPC 8 64682 01126 0
9 781583 557891
10 9 8 7 6 5 4 3 2 1
Made in the USA

A POCKET NATURALIST® GUIDE

TORONTO BIRDS

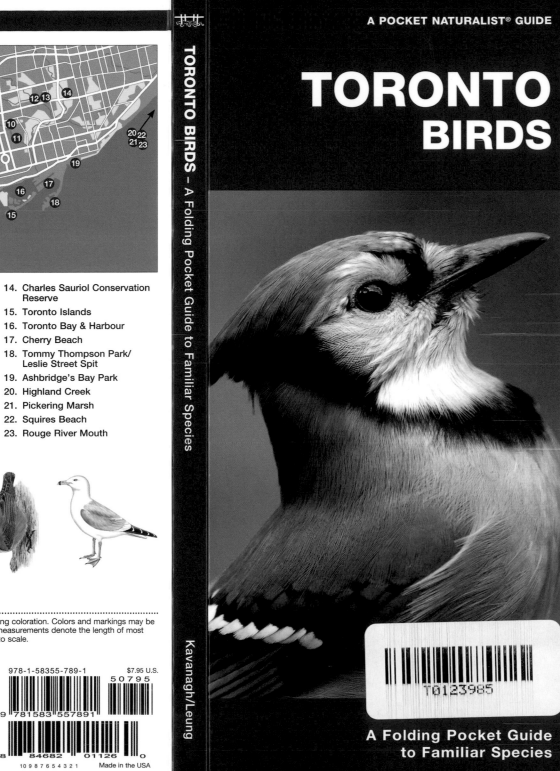

A Folding Pocket Guide to Familiar Species

TORONTO BIRDS – A Folding Pocket Guide to Familiar Species

Kavanagh/Leung

$7.95 U.S.

T0123985

WATERBIRDS & NEARSHORE BIRDS

Common Loon
Gavia immer To 3 ft. (90 cm)
Haunting call sounds like – yodel-ha-oo-oo.
Winter
Summer

Horned Grebe
Podiceps auritus To 15 in. (38 cm)
Note reddish neck and ear tufts.

Canada Goose
Branta canadensis
To 45 in. (1.14 m)

Red-necked Grebe
Podiceps grisegena
To 19 in. (48 cm)

Mute Swan
Cygnus olor To 5 ft. (1.5 m)
Introduced resident species.

Wood Duck
Aix sponsa To 20 in. (50 cm)

American Black Duck
Anas rubripes To 25 in. (63 cm)

Mallard
Anas platyrhynchos To 28 in. (70 cm)

Blue-winged Teal
Spatula discors To 16 in. (40 cm)

Green-winged Teal
Anas crecca To 15 in. (38 cm)

Northern Shoveler
Spatula clypeata To 20 in. (50 cm)
Named for its large spatulate bill.

American Wigeon
Mareca americana To 23 in. (58 cm)

WATERBIRDS & NEARSHORE BIRDS

Redhead
Aythya americana To 22 in. (55 cm)

Northern Pintail
Anas acuta To 30 in. (75 cm)

Greater Scaup
Aythya marila To 20 in. (50 cm)

Ring-necked Duck
Aythya collaris To 18 in. (45 cm)
Note white ring near bill tip.

Bufflehead
Bucephala albeola To 15 in. (38 cm)

Common Goldeneye
Bucephala clangula
To 18 in. (45 cm)

Gadwall
Mareca strepera To 21 in. (53 cm)

Red-breasted Merganser
Mergus serrator To 27 in. (68 cm)
Note prominent head crest.

Long-tailed Duck
Clangula hyemalis To 22 in. (55 cm)

Hooded Merganser
Lophodytes cucullatus
To 20 in. (50 cm)

Ruddy Duck
Oxyura jamaicensis
To 16 in. (40 cm)
Note cocked tail.

WATERBIRDS & NEARSHORE BIRDS

American Coot
Fulica americana
To 16 in. (40 cm)

Spotted Sandpiper
Actitis macularius
To 8 in. (20 cm)
Breast is spotted.

Double-crested Cormorant
Phalacrocorax auritus
To 3 ft. (90 cm)
Note orange-yellow facial skin.

American Woodcock
Scolopax minor
To 12 in. (30 cm)
Chunky, long-billed bird.

Killdeer
Charadrius vociferus
To 12 in. (30 cm)
Note two breast bands.

American Bittern
Botaurus lentiginosus
To 23 in. (58 cm)
Secretive marsh bird has a distinctive call – oonk–KA-lunk.

Wilson's Snipe
Gallinago delicata
To 12 in. (30 cm)

Common Tern
Sterna hirundo
To 15 in. (38 cm)
Note black cap and forked tail. Orange bill is black-tipped.

Green Heron
Butorides virescens
To 22 in. (55 cm)

Great Blue Heron
Ardea herodias
To 4.5 ft. (1.4 m)

Herring Gull
Larus argentatus
To 26 in. (65 cm)
Legs are pinkish.

Black-crowned Night-Heron
Nycticorax nycticorax
To 28 in. (70 cm)

Ring-billed Gull
Larus delawarensis
To 20 in. (50 cm)
Bill has dark ring.

WATERBIRDS & NEARSHORE BIRDS

Black Tern
Chlidonias niger
To 10 in. (25 cm)

Great Black-backed Gull
Larus marinus
To 32 in. (80 cm)
Told by large size and dark back.

DOVES, WOODPECKERS, ETC.

Ring-necked Pheasant
Phasianus colchicus
To 3 ft. (90 cm)

Mourning Dove
Zenaida macroura
To 13 in. (33 cm)
Call is a mournful – ooah-woo-woo-woo.

Rock Pigeon
Columba livia
To 13 in. (33 cm)

Hairy Woodpecker
Dryobates villosus
To 10 in. (25 cm)

Red-headed Woodpecker
Melanerpes erythrocephalus
To 10 in. (25 cm)

Downy Woodpecker
Dryobates pubescens
To 6 in. (15 cm)
The similar hairy woodpecker is larger and has a longer bill.

Pileated Woodpecker
Dryocopus pileatus
To 17 in. (43 cm)

Northern Flicker
Colaptes auratus
To 13 in. (33 cm)
Wing and tail linings are yellow.

Yellow-bellied Sapsucker
Sphyrapicus varius
To 9 in. (23 cm)
Drills holes in trees and feeds on the sap and insects that collect there.

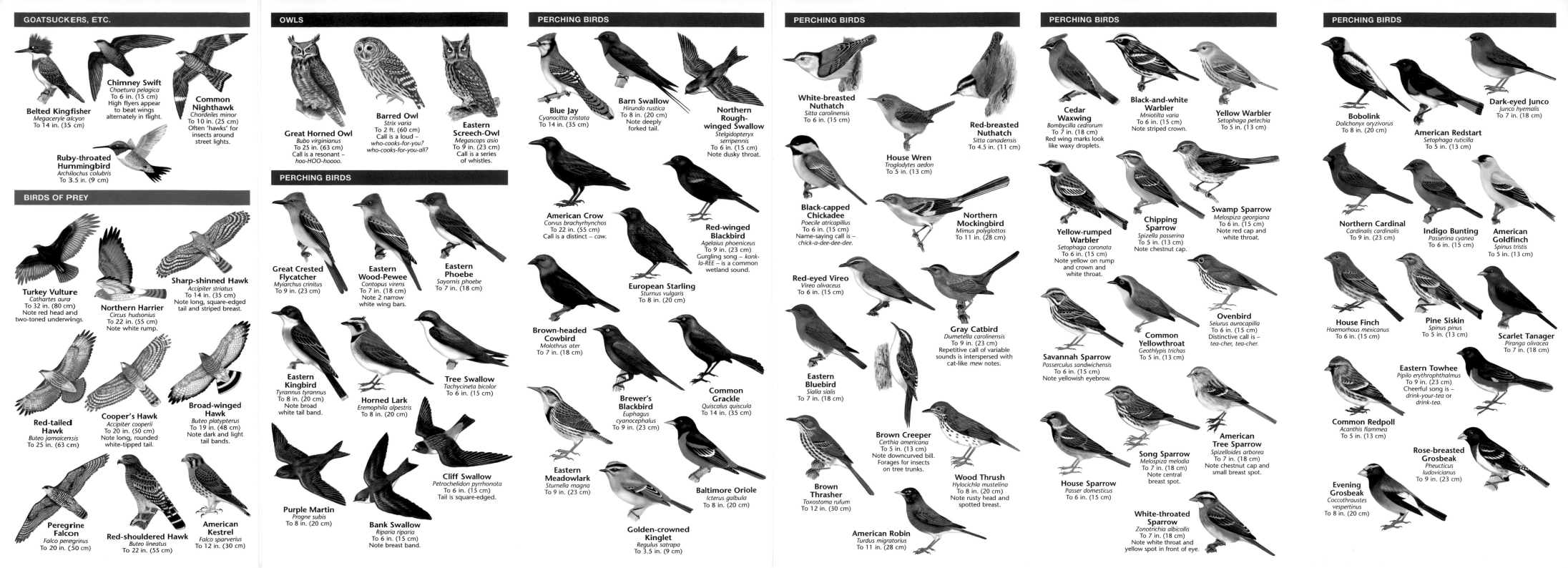

GOATSUCKERS, ETC.

Belted Kingfisher
Megaceryle alcyon
To 14 in. (35 cm)

Ruby-throated Hummingbird
Archilochus colubris
To 3.5 in. (9 cm)

Chimney Swift
Chaetura pelagica
To 6 in. (15 cm)
High flyers appear to beat wings alternately in flight.

Common Nighthawk
Chordeiles minor
To 10 in. (25 cm)
Often 'hawks' for insects around street lights.

BIRDS OF PREY

Turkey Vulture
Cathartes aura
To 32 in. (80 cm)
Note red head and two-toned underwings.

Northern Harrier
Circus hudsonius
To 22 in. (55 cm)
Note white rump.

Sharp-shinned Hawk
Accipiter striatus
To 14 in. (35 cm)
Note long, square-edged tail and striped breast.

Red-tailed Hawk
Buteo jamaicensis
To 25 in. (63 cm)

Cooper's Hawk
Accipiter cooperii
To 20 in. (50 cm)
Note long, rounded white-tipped tail.

Broad-winged Hawk
Buteo platypterus
To 19 in. (48 cm)
Note dark and light tail bands.

Peregrine Falcon
Falco peregrinus
To 20 in. (50 cm)

Red-shouldered Hawk
Buteo lineatus
To 22 in. (55 cm)

American Kestrel
Falco sparverius
To 12 in. (30 cm)

OWLS

Great Horned Owl
Bubo virginianus
To 25 in. (63 cm)
Call is a resonant –
hoo-HOO-hoooo.

Barred Owl
Strix varia
To 2 ft. (60 cm)
Call is a loud –
who-cooks-for-you?
who-cooks-for-you-all?

Eastern Screech-Owl
Megascops asio
To 9 in. (23 cm)
Call is a series of whistles.

PERCHING BIRDS

Great Crested Flycatcher
Myiarchus crinitus
To 9 in. (23 cm)

Eastern Wood-Pewee
Contopus virens
To 7 in. (18 cm)
Note 2 narrow white wing bars.

Eastern Phoebe
Sayornis phoebe
To 7 in. (18 cm)

Eastern Kingbird
Tyrannus tyrannus
To 8 in. (20 cm)
Note broad white tail band.

Horned Lark
Eremophila alpestris
To 8 in. (20 cm)

Tree Swallow
Tachycineta bicolor
To 6 in. (15 cm)

Purple Martin
Progne subis
To 8 in. (20 cm)

Bank Swallow
Riparia riparia
To 6 in. (15 cm)

Cliff Swallow
Petrochelidon pyrrhonota
To 6 in. (15 cm)
Tail is square-edged.

PERCHING BIRDS

Blue Jay
Cyanocitta cristata
To 14 in. (35 cm)

Barn Swallow
Hirundo rustica
To 8 in. (20 cm)
Note deeply forked tail.

Northern Rough-winged Swallow
Stelgidopteryx serripennis
To 6 in. (15 cm)
Note dusky throat.

American Crow
Corvus brachyrhynchos
To 22 in. (55 cm)
Call is a distinct – caw.

Red-winged Blackbird
Agelaius phoeniceus
To 9 in. (23 cm)
Gurgling song – konk-la-REE – is a common wetland sound.

Brown-headed Cowbird
Molothrus ater
To 7 in. (18 cm)

European Starling
Sturnus vulgaris
To 8 in. (20 cm)

Brewer's Blackbird
Euphagus cyanocephalus
To 9 in. (23 cm)

Common Grackle
Quiscalus quiscula
To 14 in. (35 cm)

Eastern Meadowlark
Sturnella magna
To 9 in. (23 cm)

Golden-crowned Kinglet
Regulus satrapa
To 3.5 in. (9 cm)

Baltimore Oriole
Icterus galbula
To 8 in. (20 cm)

PERCHING BIRDS

White-breasted Nuthatch
Sitta carolinensis
To 6 in. (15 cm)

Red-breasted Nuthatch
Sitta canadensis
To 4.5 in. (11 cm)

Black-capped Chickadee
Poecile atricapillus
To 6 in. (15 cm)
Name-saying call is – chick-a-dee-dee-dee.

House Wren
Troglodytes aedon
To 5 in. (13 cm)

Northern Mockingbird
Mimus polyglottos
To 11 in. (28 cm)

Red-eyed Vireo
Vireo olivaceus
To 6 in. (15 cm)

Gray Catbird
Dumetella carolinensis
To 9 in. (23 cm)
Repetitive call of variable sounds is interspersed with cat-like *mew* notes.

Eastern Bluebird
Sialia sialis
To 7 in. (18 cm)

Brown Creeper
Certhia americana
To 5 in. (13 cm)
Note downcurved bill. Forages for insects on tree trunks.

Brown Thrasher
Toxostoma rufum
To 12 in. (30 cm)

Wood Thrush
Hylocichla mustelina
To 8 in. (20 cm)
Note rusty head and spotted breast.

American Robin
Turdus migratorius
To 11 in. (28 cm)

PERCHING BIRDS

Cedar Waxwing
Bombycilla cedrorum
To 7 in. (18 cm)
Red wing marks look like waxy droplets.

Black-and-white Warbler
Mniotilta varia
To 6 in. (15 cm)
Note striped crown.

Yellow Warbler
Setophaga petechia
To 5 in. (13 cm)

Yellow-rumped Warbler
Setophaga coronata
To 6 in. (15 cm)
Note yellow on rump and crown and white throat.

Chipping Sparrow
Spizella passerina
To 5 in. (13 cm)
Note chestnut cap.

Swamp Sparrow
Melospiza georgiana
To 6 in. (15 cm)
Note red cap and white throat.

Common Yellowthroat
Geothlypis trichas
To 5 in. (13 cm)

Ovenbird
Seiurus aurocapilla
To 6 in. (15 cm)
Distinctive call is – tea-cher, tea-cher.

Savannah Sparrow
Passerculus sandwichensis
To 6 in. (15 cm)
Note yellowish eyebrow.

American Tree Sparrow
Spizelloides arborea
To 6 in. (15 cm)
Note chestnut cap and small breast spot.

Song Sparrow
Melospiza melodia
To 7 in. (18 cm)
Note central breast spot.

House Sparrow
Passer domesticus
To 6 in. (15 cm)

White-throated Sparrow
Zonotrichia albicollis
To 7 in. (18 cm)
Note white throat and yellow spot in front of eye.

PERCHING BIRDS

Bobolink
Dolichonyx oryzivorus
To 8 in. (20 cm)

American Redstart
Setophaga ruticilla
To 5 in. (13 cm)

Dark-eyed Junco
Junco hyemalis
To 7 in. (18 cm)

Northern Cardinal
Cardinalis cardinalis
To 9 in. (23 cm)

Indigo Bunting
Passerina cyanea
To 6 in. (15 cm)

American Goldfinch
Spinus tristis
To 5 in. (13 cm)

House Finch
Haemorhous mexicanus
To 6 in. (15 cm)

Pine Siskin
Spinus pinus
To 5 in. (13 cm)

Scarlet Tanager
Piranga olivacea
To 7 in. (18 cm)

Eastern Towhee
Pipilo erythrophthalmus
To 9 in. (23 cm)
Cheerful song is – drink-your-tea or drink-tea.

Common Redpoll
Acanthis flammea
To 5 in. (13 cm)

Rose-breasted Grosbeak
Pheucticus ludovicianus
To 9 in. (23 cm)

Evening Grosbeak
Coccothraustes vespertinus
To 8 in. (20 cm)